The Easy

Glenn Miller

23 classic songs for keyboard

© International Music Publications Ltd
First published in 1998 by International Music Publications Ltd
International Music Publications Ltd is a Faber Music company
Bloomsbury House 74–77 Great Russell Street London WC1B 3DA

Cover Image © Felix Man/Hulton Archive

Music arranged & processed by Barnes Music Engraving Ltd

Printed in England by Caligraving Ltd
All rights reserved

ISBN10: 0-571-52854-6
EAN13: 978-0-571-52854-7

Alice Blue Gown

Words by Joseph McCarthy / Music by Harry Tierney

Suggested Registration: Piano
Rhythm: Waltz
Tempo: ♩ = 80

In my sweet lit - tle A - lice blue

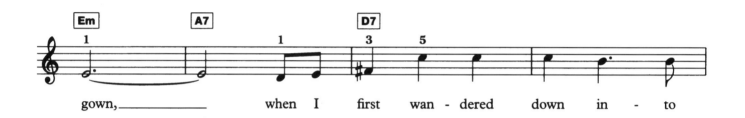

gown,_____ when I first wan - dered down in - to

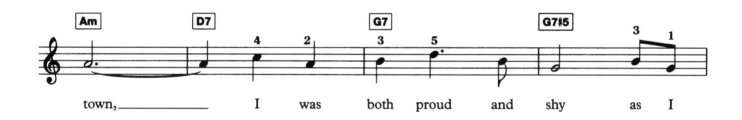

town,_____ I was both proud and shy as I

felt ev - 'ry eye, but in ev - 'ry shop win - dow I'd

'primp' pass - ing by. Then in man - ner of fash - ion I'd

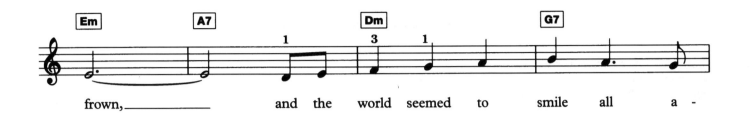

frown,_____ and the world seemed to smile all a -

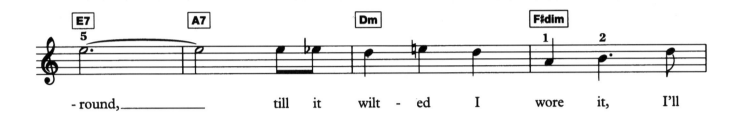

- round,_____ till it wilt - ed I wore it, I'll

al - ways a - dore it, my sweet lit - tle

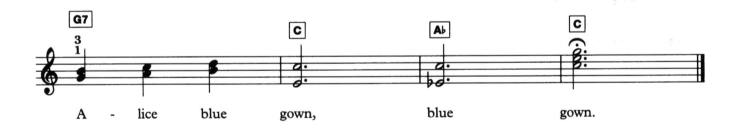

A - lice blue gown, blue gown.

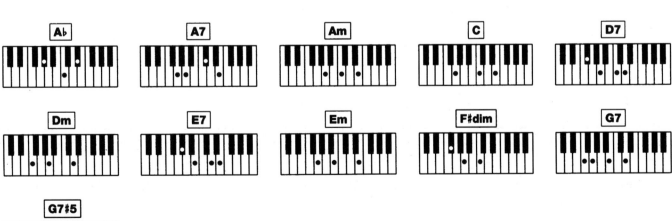

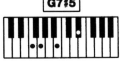

AMERICAN PATROL

Traditional

Suggested Registration: Brass
Rhythm: Swing
Tempo: ♩ = 150

AND THE ANGELS SING

Words by Johnny Mercer / Music by Ziggie Elman

Suggested Registration: Trombone
Rhythm: Swing
Tempo: ♩ = 120

At Last

Words by Mack Gordon / Music by Harry Warren

Suggested Registration: Vibraphone
Rhythm: Swing
Tempo: ♩ = 84

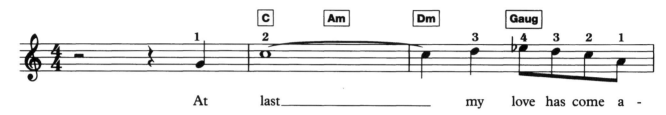

At last_____ my love has come a-

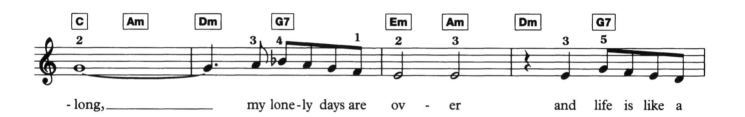

-long,_____ my lone-ly days are ov - er and life is like a

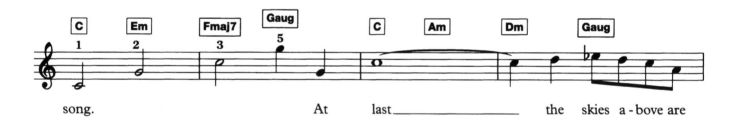

song. At last_____ the skies a-bove are

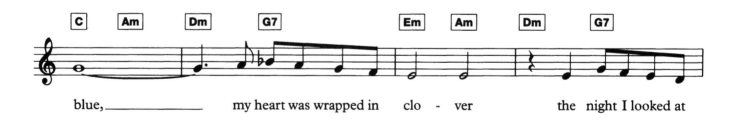

blue,_____ my heart was wrapped in clo - ver the night I looked at

you. I found a dream that I can speak to, a dream that

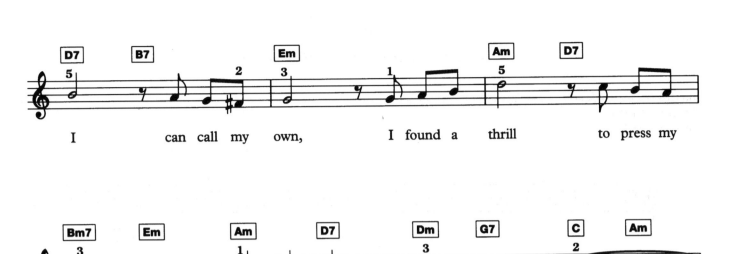

I   can call my   own,   I found a   thrill   to press my

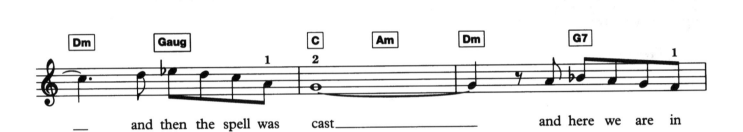

cheek   to,   a   thrill I've   ne - ver known.   You   smiled_____

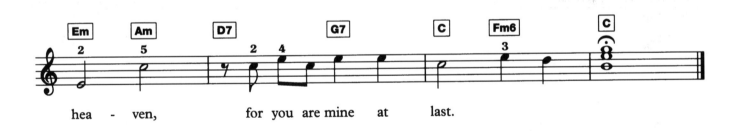

__   and then the spell was   cast_____   and here we   are   in

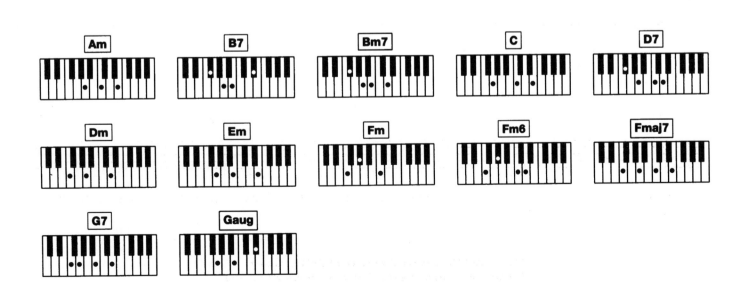

hea - ven,   for you are mine   at   last.

Chattanooga Choo Choo

Words by Mack Gordon / Music by Harry Warren

Suggested Registration: Clarinet
Rhythm: 8 Beat
Tempo: ♩ = 128

© 1941 & 1998 EMI Catalogue Partnership and EMI Feist Catalog Inc, USA
Worldwide print rights controlled by Warner Bros Publications Inc/IMP Ltd

Don't Sit Under The Apple Tree

Words and Music by Lew Brown, Charles Tobias and Sam Stept

Suggested Registration: Vibraphone / Jazz Guitar
Rhythm: Jazz Swing
Tempo: ♩ = 140

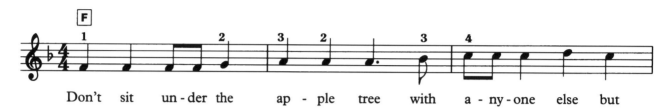

Don't sit un-der the ap-ple tree with a-ny-one else but

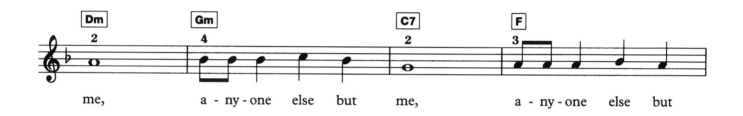

me, a-ny-one else but me, a-ny-one else but

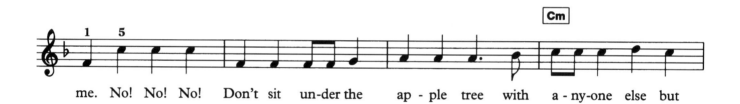

me. No! No! No! Don't sit un-der the ap-ple tree with a-ny-one else but

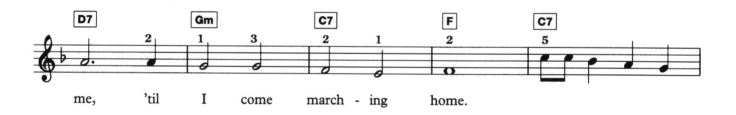

me, 'til I come march-ing home.

Don't go walk-in' down lov-er's lane with a-ny-one else but me,

a-ny-one else but me, a-ny-one else but me. No! No! No!

Elmer's Tune

Words and Music by Elmer Albrecht, Sammy Gallop and Dick Jurgens

Suggested Registration: Trumpet
Rhythm: Slow Rock
Tempo: ♩ = 94

Why are the stars al - ways wink-in' and blink-in' a - bove? What makes a

fel - low start think-in' of fall-in' in love?_ It's not the sea-son, the rea-son is

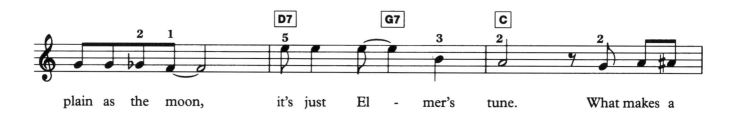

plain as the moon, it's just El - mer's tune. What makes a

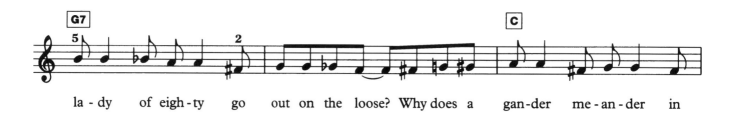

la - dy of eigh-ty go out on the loose? Why does a gan-der me-an-der in

search of a goose? What puts the kick in a chick-en, the ma-gic of June?

It's just El - mer's tune.____ Lis - ten,__ lis - ten__

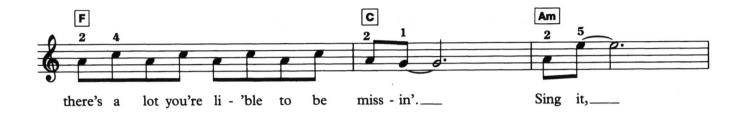

there's a lot you're li - 'ble to be miss - in'.___ Sing it,___

swing it___ a - ny old way and a - ny old time._ The hur - dy

gur - dies, the bird - ies, the 'cap' on the beat,___ the can - dy

ma-ker, the ba-ker, the man in the street, the ci - ty charm-er, the farm-er, the

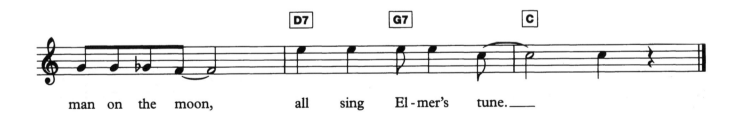

man on the moon, all sing El - mer's tune.___

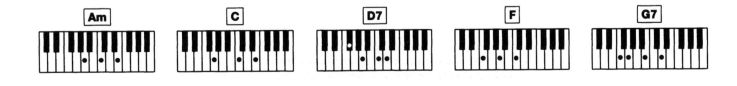

HEAR MY SONG, VIOLETTA

Original Words by Othmar Klose, English Words by Harry S Pepper / Music by Othmar Klose and Rudolf Luckesch

Suggested Registration: Violin
Rhythm: Tango
Tempo: ♩ = 110

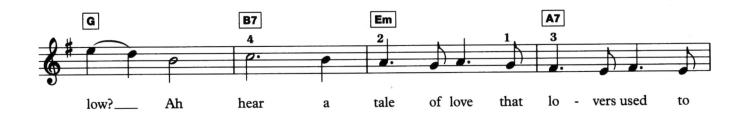

low?___ Ah hear a tale of love that lo - vers used to

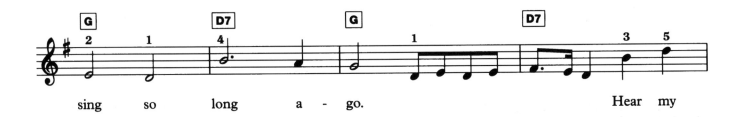

sing so long a - go. Hear my

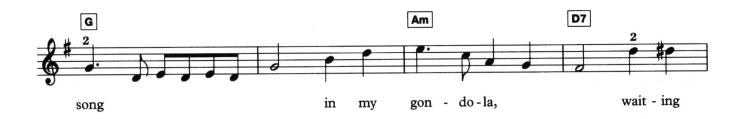

song in my gon - do - la, wait - ing

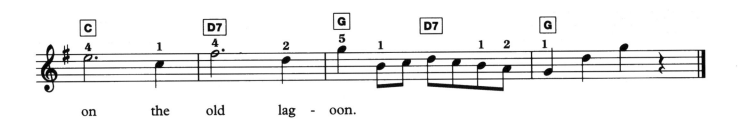

on the old lag - oon.

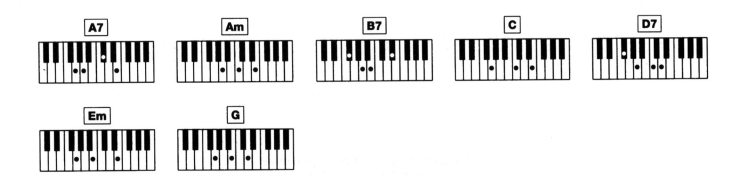

I Know Why And So Do You

Words by Mack Gordon / Music by Harry Warren

Suggested Registration: Clarinet
Rhythm: Swing
Tempo: ♩ = 80

Why do rob-ins sing   in De - cem - ber,   long be-fore the spring-time is

due,   and   e - ven though it's snow-ing,   vi - o - lets are grow-ing?

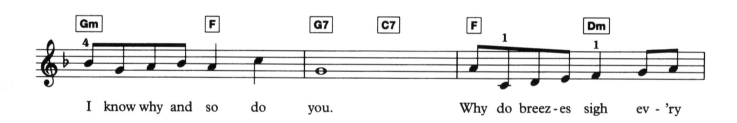

I know why and so   do   you.   Why do breez-es sigh ev - 'ry

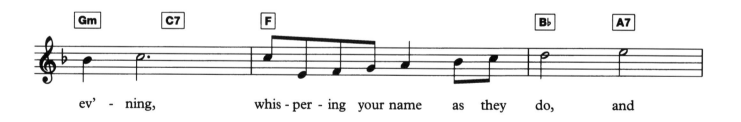

ev' - ning,   whis-per-ing your name   as they   do,   and

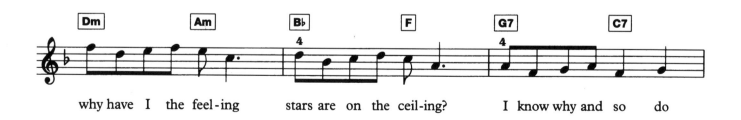

why have I the feel-ing   stars are on the ceil-ing?   I know why and so   do

In The Mood

Words and Music by Joe Garland

Suggested Registration: Tenor Saxophone
Rhythm: Swing
Tempo: ♩ = 120

Who's the liv-in' dol-ly with the beau-ti-ful eyes? What a pair o' lips, I'd like to

try 'em for size.__ I'll just tell her, 'Ba-by, won't you swing it with me?'__

Hope she tells me may-be, what a wing it will be.__ So I said po-lite-ly, 'Dar-lin',

may I in-trude?' She said, 'Don't keep me wait-ing when I'm in the mood.'

First I held her light-ly, and we start-ed to dance, then I held her tight-ly, what a

dream-y ro-mance, and I said, 'Hey ba-by, it's a quart-er to three,

It Happened In Sun Valley

Words by Mack Gordon / Music by Harry Warren

Suggested Registration: Jazz Guitar
Rhythm: Cha-Cha
Tempo: ♩ = 116

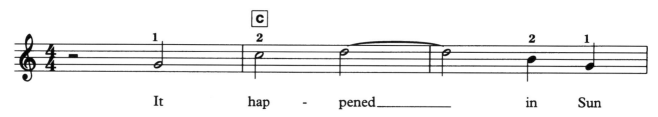

It hap - pened _____ in Sun

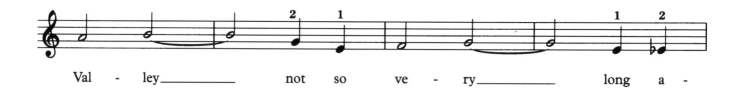

Val - ley _____ not so ve - ry _____ long a -

- go, there were sun - beams _____ in the

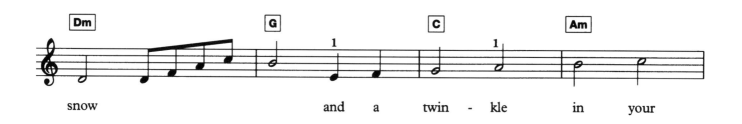

snow and a twin - kle in your

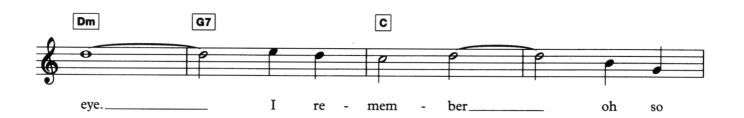

eye. _____ I re - mem - ber _____ oh so

clear - ly_____ , that you near - ly_____ passed me

Dm   **G7**   **Am**   **Fm**

by,   then it hap - pened in Sun

C   **A7**   **Dm**

Val - ley_____ when you slipped and fell and

G7   **C**   **Fm**   **C**

so did I.

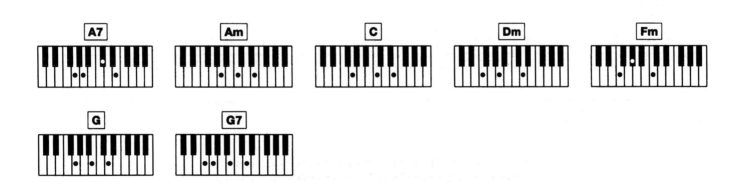

Johnson Rag

Words by Jack Lawrence / Music by Guy Hall and Henry Kleinkauf

Suggested Registration: Piano
Rhythm: Swing
Tempo: ♩ = 142

Hep! Hep!_____ There goes the John - son rag.__ Hoy!

Hoy!_____ There goes the lat - est rag.__ Ho! Ho!_____ It real - ly

is - n't a gag.__ Hep! Hep!_____ There goes the John - son rag.__ Jump!

Jump!_____ Don't let your left foot drag.__ Jeep! Jeep!_____ It's like a

game of tag.__ Juke! Juke!_____ It's e - ven good for a stag.__ Jump!

Jump!_____ And do the John - son rag._____ If you're feel - in'

in the groove it sends you out of the world.___

Fun - ny how it makes you move I don't want to coax,__ but

don't be a 'mokes'. Zig! Zig!_____ Then add a Zig! Zig! Sag!__ Zoop!

Zoop!_____ Just let your should - ers wag.__ Zoom! Zoom!_____ And now it's

right in the bag.__ Get hep, and get hap - py with the John - son rag.__

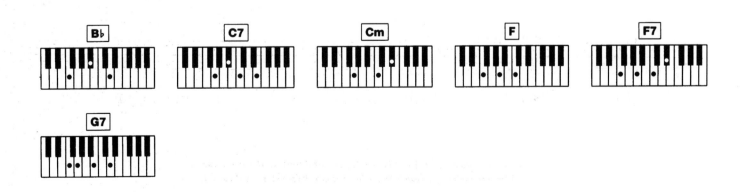

King Porter Stomp

Music by Ferd 'Jelly Roll' Morton, Arranged by Sonny Burke and Sid Robin

Suggested Registration: Honky Tonk Piano
Rhythm: Swing
Tempo: ♩ = 120

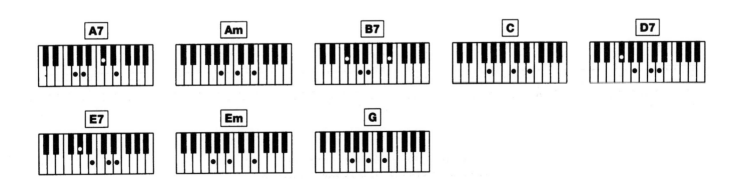

LITTLE BROWN JUG

Music by R A Eastburn

Suggested Registration: Saxophone
Rhythm: Swing
Tempo: ♩ = 114

Moonlight Serenade

Words by Mitchell Parish / Music by Glenn Miller

Suggested Registration: Saxophone
Rhythm: Slow Swing
Tempo: ♩ = 72

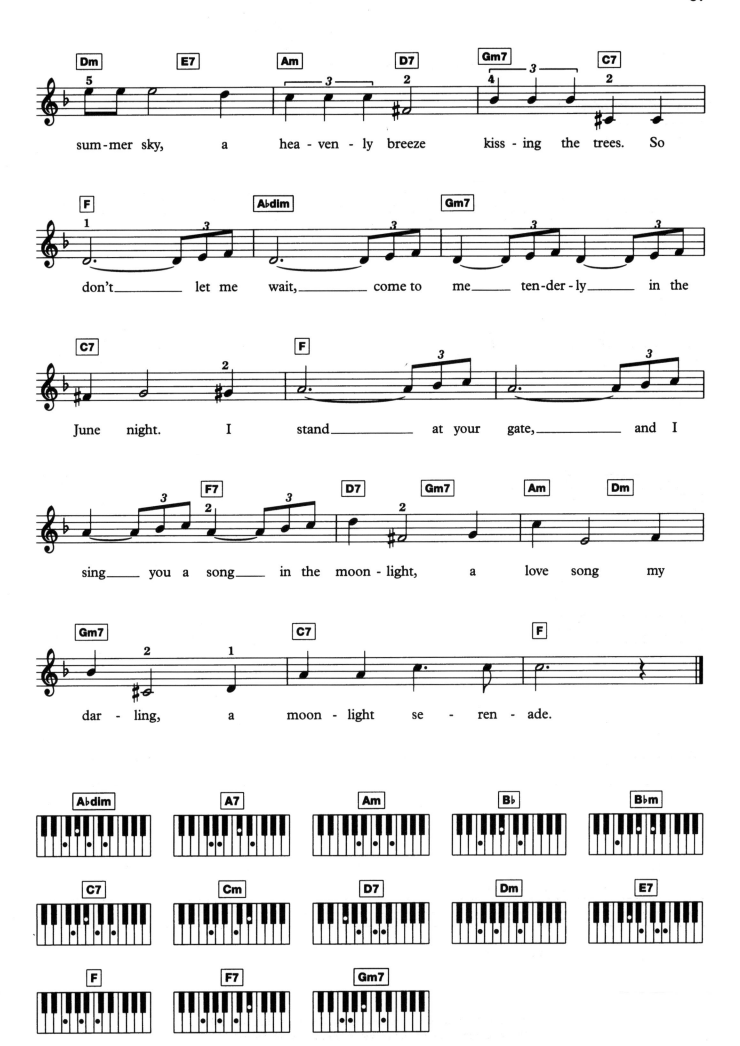

My Blue Heaven

Words by George Whiting / Music by Walter Donaldson

Suggested Registration: Muted Trumpet
Rhythm: Swing
Tempo: ♩ = 154

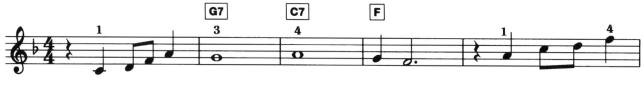

When whip-poor-wills

call_____ and ev-'ning is nigh,_____ I hur-ry to

my blue hea - ven. A turn to the

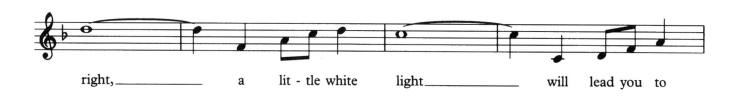

right,_____ a lit-tle white light_____ will lead you to

my blue hea - ven. You'll see a

smil - ing face, a fire - place, a co - zy room,_____ a

lit - tle nest that's nest - led where the ro - ses bloom. Just Mol-lie and

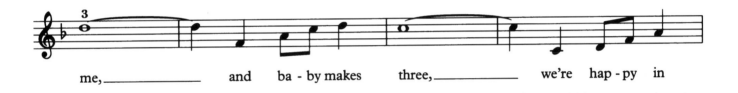

me,_____ and ba - by makes three,_____ we're hap - py in

my blue hea - ven._____

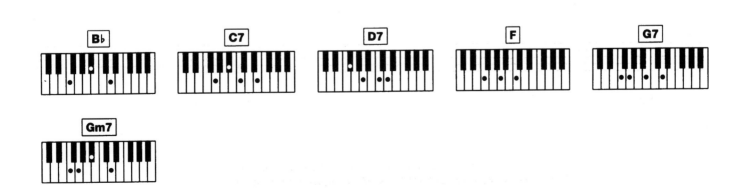

My Guy's Come Back

Words by Ray McKinley / Music by Mel Powell

Suggested Registration: Trumpet
Rhythm: Jazz Swing
Tempo: ♩ = 140

Some - thin's cook-in' that -'ll   rate an o - va-tion, will you   note   that   I am in a

state of e - la-tion, won't you   call   the press in, 'cos I've   got a quo - ta-tion, and I'll

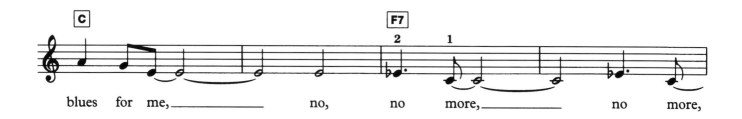

tell   the na-tion that my   guy's come back.   No   more_____

blues   for   me,_____   no,   no   more,_____   no   more,

just good_____

news for me,_____ just good news_____ in store.

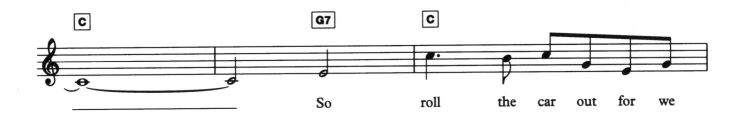

_____ So roll the car out for we

got-ta get mov-in', let us have a star out for my guy is a-prov-in' ev-'ry

time, we're step-pin' out we real-ly get groov-in', and the life's im-prov-in' for my

guy's come back._

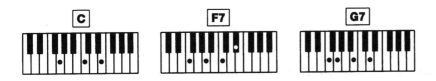

Pennsylvania 6-5000

Words by Carl Sigman / Music by Jerry Gray

Suggested Registration: Brass
Rhythm: Swing
Tempo: ♩ = 128

Num-bers I've got by the doz - en,___ ev - 'ry-one's un-cle and

cou - sin,___ but I can't live with-out buzz - in'___ Penn-syl-van-ia

six, five thous-and. I've got a sweet-ie I know there,_

some - one who sets me a - glow there,_ gives me the sweet-est 'hel -

-lo there' Penn-syl-van-ia six, five thous-and. We don't say 'How

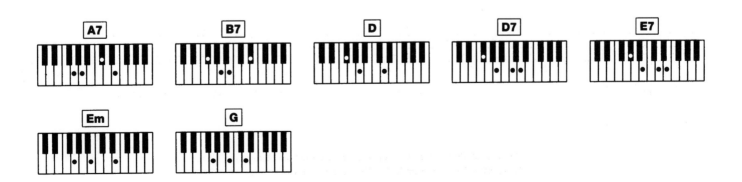

Running Wild

Words by Joe Gray and Leo Wood / Music by Arthur Harrington Gibbs

Suggested Registration: Brass
Rhythm: Swing
Tempo: ♩ = 150

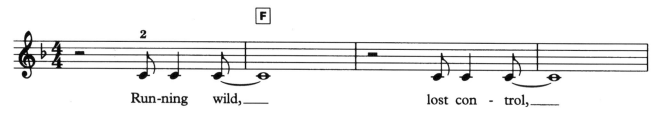

Run-ning wild,____ lost con - trol,____

run-ning wild,____ migh - ty bold,____

feel - ing gay,____ reck - less too.____

Care-free mind____ all the time,____ ne - ver blue,____

al - way's goin', ___   don't know where, ___

al - way's showin' __   I don't care. ____

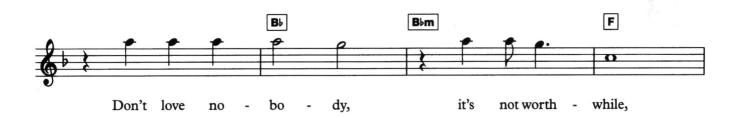

Don't love no - bo - dy,   it's not worth - while,

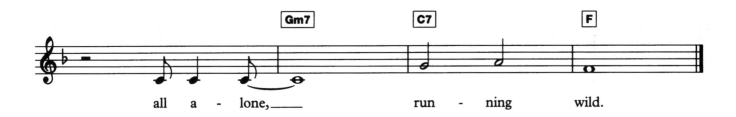

all a - lone, ____   run - ning wild.

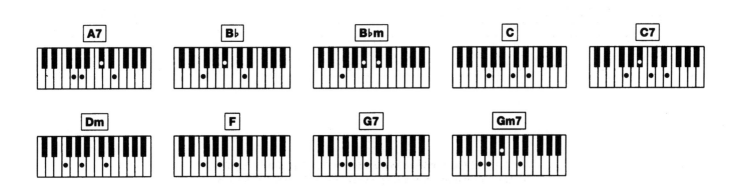

St Louis Blues

Music by W C Handy

Suggested Registration: Brass
Rhythm: Shuffle or Swing
Tempo: ♩ = 98

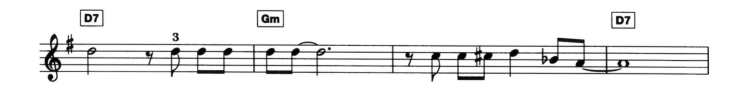

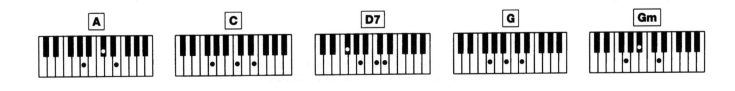

Stairway To The Stars

Words by Mitchell Parish / Music by Matty Malneck and Frank Signorelli

Suggested Registration: Electric Piano
Rhythm: Swing
Tempo: ♩ = 80

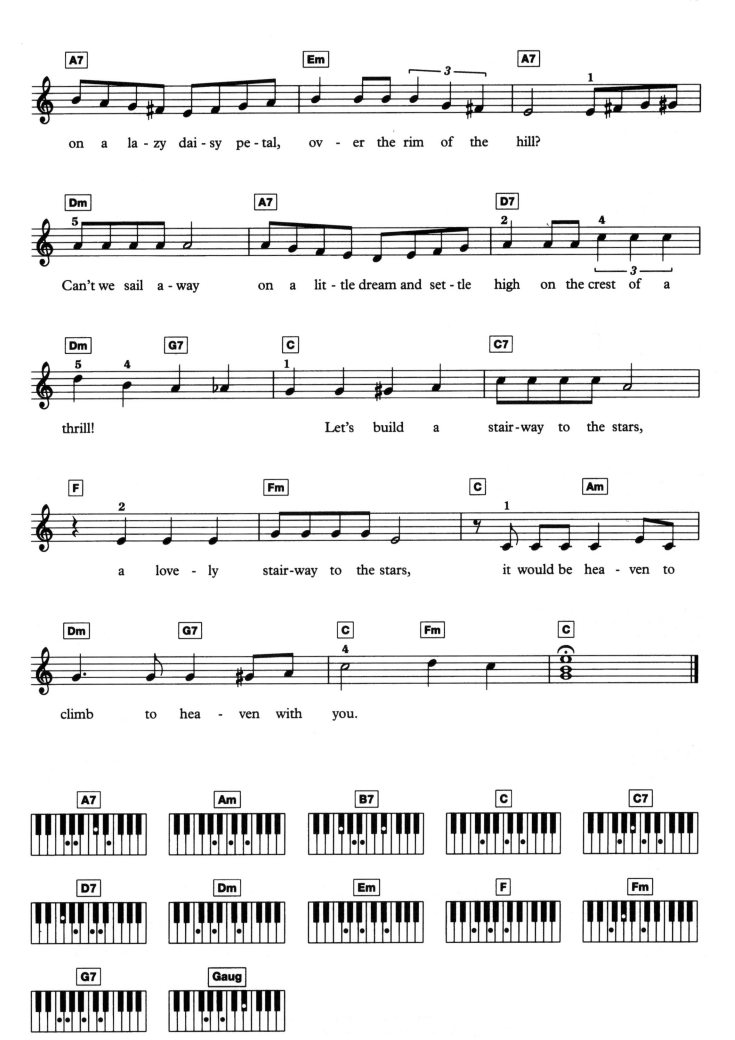

Sunrise Serenade

Words by Jack Lawrence / Music by Frankie Carle

Suggested Registration: Vibraphone
Rhythm: Slow Rock
Tempo: ♩ = 76

Good morn-in', good morn-in' you sleep-y head, it's

dawn-in', stop yawn-in' get out of that bed.__ Say the air is soft as silk, it's time to

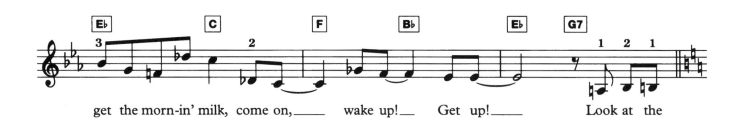

get the morn-in' milk, come on,____ wake up!__ Get up!____ Look at the

grass, sil-ver in the sun, hea-vy with the dew, look at the

buds, you can al-most see how they're break-in' thro'.____ Look at the

Wonderful One

Words by Dorothy Terriss / Music by Paul Whiteman, Ferde Grofé and Marshall Neilan

Suggested Registration: Strings
Rhythm: Waltz
Tempo: ♩ = 90

My won - der - ful one, when - ev - er I'm

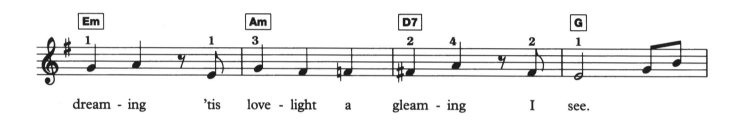

dream - ing 'tis love - light a gleam - ing I see.

My won - der - ful one, to my heart I would

fold you, for - ev - er to hold you to___ me.

Though bright be the light of the stars shin - ing

o'er me and gold - en the rays of the

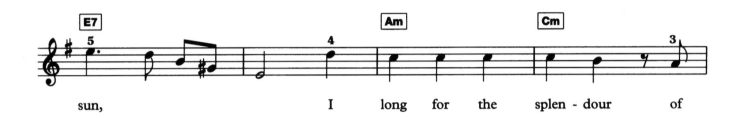

sun, I long for the splen - dour of

eyes true and ten - der, my won - der - ful,

won - der - ful one.

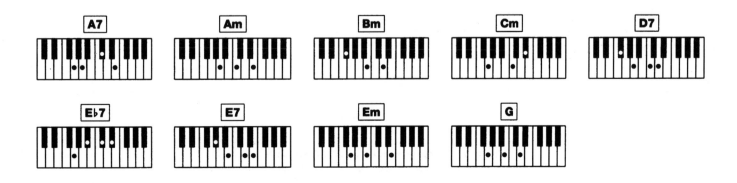

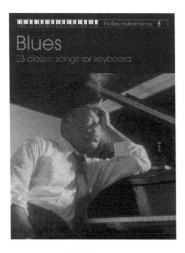
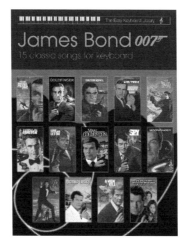

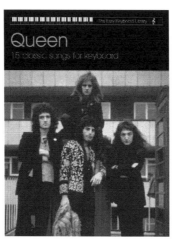